SENDING THE BODY OUT

A N N E   V A L L E Y   F O X
SENDING THE BODY OUT

Zephyr Press

Copyright © 1986 by Anne Valley Fox
All rights reserved.
First edition.
Printed in the United States of America.

"Snake" and "Certainty" first appeared in
The American Voice. *Sending the Body Out* was nominated
for the Western States Book Awards, 1985.

Cover art from an original cyanotype by Nancy Sutor.
Design by Ed Hogan.

*Publication of this book was assisted by a grant from the
Massachusetts Council on the Arts and Humanities.*

ISBN 0-939010-08-9
Library of Congress Catalogue Card No. 86-50252

ZEPHYR PRESS
13 Robinson Street
Somerville, Massachusetts 02145

*for Kosai Kobari
Ilmars Purens and
all my family*

"You go around it in an hour and a half — you begin to recognize that your identity is with that whole thing. And that makes a change. You look down there and you can't imagine how many borders and boundaries you cross, again and again and again. And you don't even see them! From where you see it the thing is a whole, and it's so beautiful. And you recall, standing out there, the spectacle that went before your eyes. Because you're no longer inside something with a window looking out at a picture — now you're out there, and there are no limits to it, there are no frames, there are no boundaries...."

— *Russell L. Schweickart, Apollo 9 pilot testing lunar module in earth orbit, March 1969*

Commitment

Ten steps into the woods and light behind you
puckers into a scar above the treetops
Sunlight flowing directly down is bathing
needles erect as the hairs on your limbs
There were signs   yes   sporadically flashing
but no preparation for this   You left
the others asleep in their beds   enveloped in
bands of dream   Your body is streaming
with fertile rivers   Your steps are patterned
yet no one has gone here — what flies
before you?   Lavish decay stirred underfoot
expands the nostrils — your own body stripped
of odor despite the rose at its center   When
have you ever been free before?   or utterly
given over!   Feet spring lightly against
the ground   you laugh as you run   vaulting
saplings   weaving through trees   ravenous
for truth

Waking

In sleep there are stairs   knives   sirens
you can't help this   you roll in your shell
in the sea   Your dreams congeal like gumtrees
and smoke   blotching the blue   Frightened
you go to the devil's bed and let him undo
your buttons   He tells you he has been mis-
understood   his kisses blister   you long for
obliteration

Without waking you've moved into town   rented
a room   enrolled in Jewelry and Basic Computer
The government sends you compensation   you
drink with friends who feed your despair with
fiendish laughter — one thing leads to another
Climbing the stairs you ask how much higher —
you no longer care where you're going

If you would wake   Aurora whispers   *something
must be returned to the night*   Mounting
the steps you receive the knives and sirens into
your body   turning back fear   your protective
blindness   You wake to a subtle change in the
weather   Something is needing you here : lay
a fire   wash a pot   put something in it   and late
in the day you may pause to feel the gathering
darkness   Evening travels under your skin   winds
blowing through stellar cells   between
your tissues   you sleep from now on with
riverbed stones weighting your eyelids
Lifting them carefully off at dawn you practice
waking empty

Rooms

Certain rooms you walk into and feel
they are yours   Because of the way the sun
slants in or an odd-shaped nook in the back
or the rumor that an artistic lunatic once
lived here   Often these rooms come with peeling
linoleum stains on the carpet dictating where
you will put the dresser a pair of spoons
cracked mascara or shoulderpads left in a drawer
This sort of place tends to show up when
you're in transition its very existence
offering reassurance   You pay the rent with
the grocery money and haul a bucket of paint
up a ladder   Later you set about hanging
posters arranging fetishes painting the bathroom
rose or black — personal touches to help you
believe it is yours

Election year   "The homeless have as much
right to vote as anyone else" a Washington lawyer
is saying over the radio   "I really prefer
to rent to couples" the widow confides "especially
if they own some furniture"   Her cast-off Frigidaire
shudders over your shoulder — it purrs and quakes
in its sleep like a cat   Home is what you bring
to it then?   You bring two lamps a Korean
dish drainer boxes of books an overstuffed
chair garbage bags packed with winter sweaters —
and damn if you don't feel at home in this place!
Last year you slept in a greenhouse under a
blanket of stars : whenever it rained you pushed
the bed to the spot in the room where the roof
wouldn't leak in your face

Winter cuts with a double edge   Did the vote
you cast make a difference?   You need your nest
in a big way now   and sometimes you loathe it
for all those refinements which always elude you
This is when you may take in a stray — a bag
of animal bones   or maybe a fugitive packing his
life down to Matamoras chased by recurring dreams
This is when you may sit in your armchair com-
puting defects   The rooms like neglected wives
no longer even try to seduce you :   chipped
walls   crooked doorframes   weather-stained
drapes   icy closets (the Gas Company's getting
away with murder) — besides there's your skin
rash   the paranoid fears plaguing you lately
you're yelling too much at the kids

This is not the end   you say   but a trend
attached to a season   Things could be worse
Somewhere there must be a room you will love
You fill the feeder at the window   offering
the birds who were left behind cranberries
for Thanksgiving

Absolution

Answer the door   The face he shows you
is scarred from kissing rocky ground
You drop to your knees   The last stranger
who stayed at this inn rode out with a landscape
of robbers and maidens coupling between his
shoulders   Make no mistake : sending the body out
like a rocket without a message without a
blessing landed you here in this graveyard
Turned-back children convene in the bellies
of clouds   From every corner remorse overcomes
moaning and cursing and prayer all in tongues

When the last of your grief is expressed from
the body the god comes in   He sits in the place
where you've matted the grass   blades
springing back just over the ground   his hands
are lifting like tropical leaves receiving
rain   His hands are the children's trampolines
and a drifter's highways   steelworkers toil
aloft in a palm and a widow thinks it's her bungalow
on Maiden Lane   You follow them into those hands —
one pulse pumps up your heart for a lifetime
Nothing appears the same anymore   Like
children and plants the body forgives   and goes
out again   its naves all hung with jewels

The Fisherman's Wife

He goes out   For months you roll in your hollowed
bed as he on the water — wake in the night with
hands plunged for rudders between your thighs
He dreams golden circles   the deepsea creature's
dim recollection of sunlight   He comes home
his heart is weighted with water   hair silver
scaled and though he is salt blind and coarse
as the gull's throat   you know him

He bathes for you   your foaming hands are voracious
He comes home   his tongue iced with salt   you are
hot and steaming for him like new potatoes
His pores open rich with fish for many days
they swarm out over your body   At first your touch
burns him strangely like jagged grass — at first
he doesn't speak   deafened by grunts of the moon
He comes home and calls you Agua...Agua...until
he recovers the textures of flesh — and then
the weaving and staining of limbs!

You drink him helplessly as one who drowns
At night through the darkness he drifts down
to the water to wash himself   You dig your garden
He sinks no hooks for the watery mouths of
imagined others   you know nothing of distances
traveled between stars or the dazzling choker
a siren wears at her throat   He comes home
and you draw him around you as folds of silk
Oxygen kisses ease him out of a deep sleep
His thrust is lightning   you're liquified diamond
The fourth night or the fifth   he gives you seed

You carry it firmly up and down mountains steep
with work for the clean black months he rides
the water   He comes home and at first he doesn't
know you — your eyes are impossible as early
morning   His voice erupts like foghorns webbed
to the sea...

On the third day you wake easy   His hands and
lips have remembered a rhythm distinct from
the waves   and you have recovered his name : Peter...
Jonah...Ulysses!   Over and over it blows from
your lips   He sails away   You plant yourself in
the deep turning doors of the ground   Your
fisherman gone to his mistress — for many months
you gauge his approach through the fog's
swollen throat

Imminence
(for Dirk)

At first you do nothing   thinking it may
go away   it may not be yours   you leave the room
and return many times surprised to see it

You live in the house as sympathetic strangers
You are the one who opens and closes the
airshafts   perfecting timing by degrees   until
the day he rides away   his children stirred
to see him go   braving the dark and the
weather   The bird taps again at the window
You step to the glass and stare :   Why have you
come?   What will you carry away?   Your
questions tangle and scratch the panes   perhaps
because of the crack in the egg standing
on end at your center   Sometimes the rooms
are empty   sometimes they boil with brawling
creatures   You talk to yourself in sign
language   This is surprisingly satisfying
a kind of pregnancy   no one expects you to
say anything or to make but one sound
There's no turning back   you know that if you
neglect to use it your throat will ache with
an unlisted sickness   The bird in the window
doesn't sing   but if you open   your house will be
flooded with music   You close your eyes :
The man lost his nerve in the woods   and
something wrapped its feathered weightlessness
tight around him clinging all night   He
felt he no longer wanted the world but only
a small corner — too late : desire repeated
ensnares the soul

Fearing the creature is trapped in yourself
you question your being—the one verity
Changing your clothes you stand at the mirror
You change again   Again he hurls himself at the
window   You tear off the flowered housecoat
Open and it may pluck out your eyes   smother
the children   or what if it freezes and drops
dead in the garden?   You know that to open
will break a spell   and because you have not lived
flawlessly   without delusion   you are afraid
You draw a bedsheet across your back   clutching
your breast   a terrible storm   light and black
blazing winds and vats of stillness raging
inside

The children gather   The girl says yes   let's
open the window   the boy warns against it   baby
spins his rainbow top on the kitchen floor
Something inside you demands release   Freeing
the latch you eye the bird through shining
glass   Your heart pounds like the law at the
door   The bird is a flame in the window   "Do
as you choose!" (he sings now to soothe you)
"—your windows   my friend   have never kept me
out"

Space

When he's in the shower you reach for your own
body you know it's the same as weeping you weep
because we are all planets gashing the heavens
slender threads fireflies flickering   Saturday
mornings you want breakfast with orchids on
the sunporch you want to live with him you want
kisses like fresh strawberries always you want
to go hand in hand   But it's not like that —
vast spaces stretching inside his eyes are
distant stars

Mail

The urge to collapse dragging your knees
ankles wobbling on tiny bones   October mornings
you walk the lane toward the mailbox
Eskimo cries out into the whiteness and
lashes his dogs   Chinese girls of your class
bound their feet   shackling the preposition
The burden is your years on earth and the chaff
you haul in your basket

Mailbox puts out its silver tongue   you
stuff it with envelopes puffed like loaves
of bread still rising   You lift the flag
circling back the long way home   Blood
creaks when it starts to flow like ice-mantled
rivers stretching toward sun

And you are neither Eskimo nor Chinese patrician
bound to abandoned centuries   Memory
serves you   Bodies are gardens   Children
are fountains of God and God is a kingdom
of fire   water   music   You draw your loved ones
into your body   rock them close   let them pass
through you   Bound by indeterminate ambits
of thorned bushes one to another   You are
the lane   you are the thorn   you are the loaf
and the morning mail soaring out in a circle

Dispassion

Being a stranger to this part of the country
he asks for your help with the landscaping
You understand he means something more — the
geographical rise and fall of feeling   This
kind of knowing he calls intuition   females
are gifted   and chasms exist between men
and women   This is a question   your answer
is changing   One thing he doesn't yet
comprehend is how with his sex he has ploughed
you open and now you need to surround him

He speaks in abstractions like bones clacking
outside the body   Rutting in flesh you exalt
and betray it in alternate stages   He doesn't
feel how you have been shattered and pieced back
together   It pleases him how you can read him
You see that he lives in a golden cage and
various females plot to release him   your
intuition is simply a chord striking inside —
the chasm between you is deep more than wide

You offer a story into the night   The heroine's
horses are out of control   she is gripping
the reins and lashing commands through a muted
terrain hauled through translucent snow
You tell this tale with a new dispassion : loving
the driver   horses   wolves   — while all of it
seems to be floating out windows   dispersing

When finally you sleep you dream your fingers
are turning over the leaves on a tree   one
by one   "I buried those feelings" he mutters
through sleep   "so deep I hardly know them"

At breakfast he tells you a story   He'd been
in Hawaii for several weeks   the job was completed
but he stayed on   depressed and angry   watching
the water   Along came a Japanese fisherman
casting his shawl of handmade nets into the sea
wirey and brown   his skull brushed with a white
bristle   the flow of his movements illustrating
contentment   At last the mourner arose and waded
into the water   The old man gestured to lift
a corner — they hauled and stretched together up to the waist
in silence   At sunset the fisherman folded his
nets back over his shoulders   bowing and waving before
turning home with his buckets of fish

The restaurant murals are dark-skinned workers
with powerful hands and mine-shaft eyes   clothed
in primary colors   You look at his mouth without
needing to kiss it

In sunlight walking slowly he says   "The bars
of my cage may be wide enough to slip through..."
You touch his hand   Too often before you
succumbed to temptation   breaking into a man's
prison and maybe then he wouldn't come out   or
you became attached to the rooms   or he left
the door swinging open

Saying goodbye you are easing through the bars
of your bodies   Men and women cannot save each
other — this much you know — but there are discreet
gifts : his fisherman   snow   joy in the body
runaway horses vaulting the chasms between us

Circles
(for Ezra)

      The child says "Why have you changed?
You don't act happy!   Here comes my dad
up the road"   Root fibers grope deeper
You answer that there are kinds of love
his father is not your father   He takes this
in   turns it over   sucking moisture through
grains of soil   Clouds rushing into each other
crash and regather   collapsed creations
transforming chambers of immaterial bodies
Flood   plague   eruption   ruin — you come up
purged   wrapped in diaphanous strips of history
one leg floating above the ground   the other
plumbing   Lungs want to burst — crazed
singing in seething streets!   Father! you shout
I am falling!   Son   you confide   I am not
your mother!   Earth embracing   sky bathing
I'll stand by your life as you strengthen —
expanding   contracting   my darling child   we're
changing places

Flying

Given to reading and drawing   the boy
had to be prodded to eat — except for breakfast
He woke hungry because in the night he left
his body and went flying   One day his mother
came home to find him watching tv with the
sound turned off and a rope tied to the
overhead fixture knotted around his neck
The next day she sent the child to her
psychiatrist   who soon told the boy he must
stop his dream flying   "Why?" queried the boy
(it had taken him a long time to learn it)
The doctor asked him what he wanted to get
away from   "Nothing really" the boy reflected
"I just love to fly"

His flights tapered off as he grew — though
once on the 4th of July he flew up into the
fireworks over the high school and wound a path
among explosions in satin trails of every
conceivable color   Cold sparks leapt from his
toes through the top of his head and he'd never
felt better   The Colonists must have felt this fine
winning their independence   he thought flying —
a gross deformation of nature for one creature
to dominate another

A girl fell in love with his delicate fingers
and tapered teeth and became his wife   When he
went to art school   she went to work as a dental
assistant   bringing home pairs of plaster of
paris teeth to show him   One night he got up

and painted a set with enamel cartoons
His flights of fancy dismayed his wife   but she
became a little more like him   and after art school
he landed a job as a medical illustrator   Once
in a dream he took her flying   She tried to
enjoy it but fear of heights overwhelmed her desire
to please and she begged him to set her down
in a parking lot

His mother described her son and his wife
to her bridge partners as "a pair of oddballs"
But some years later   on her deathbed   when
flesh was swollen purple around her wedding
ring   although she'd never pampered her husband
while he was living   she died refusing to
let them saw it off

Certainty

You can't get out of this life   its leafy
shadows catching you up like a carriage
Invisible root systems plumbing the earth
are your dread   your conviction   your longing
for sea   for hyperbole   and the lenient arms
of small children

You think so long as you put on your shoes
and walk out into the snow... set down
your hammer and knock on the locked door
that something is changing   But whatever you do
your life goes on rolling from summit to valley
light to dusk   you are animal husk   delicate
fossil drifting toward silt

Try to escape it!   Climb on a chair and loop
your rope from a ceiling beam — the dog
pushes in trailed by the mailman bringing you
word : you've won the grocer's lottery $100
in meat and butter

Or the girl leaving home in search of her life
ineluctably falling in love with her history
professor   The lines of his argument twist
off the page becoming her cyclone   She travels
above the treetops   To bury herself in his bristled
years she forgets she began on a wider current
of ectoplasmic desire   She tells herself now
she has entered her life   that these are his
arms   that she's safe in his broad-shouldered
heart   She feels she's been put in a cage   rocked

in a boat   She thinks to insist makes it so
She thinks she moves from place to place   owns
things   wins and loses   and rarely recalls
how she swayed in the limbs of her grandfather
oak   breezes singing the body

It's good to wear shoes and walk out into the snow
Good to take up   then set down the hammer   luck
to be found by your dog   Years maybe lifetimes
later you laugh at yourself : did you ever for an
instant really leave that tree?

Snake

Caretaking somebody's home you avoid the snake
sleeping under a handtowel in the terrarium
But after some weeks   dreamsnake curled in the
tip of the spine thirsting to lap at the skull's
pond   brings a message : *give me water*
You snap on the light   The real constrictor
lies with his throat collapsed against the
basin   He draws back as you pour springwater
into his bowl   glaring through you with tiny
lusterless eyes   He won't drink in your presence
but later you see he has quenched his thirst
in great quantity   later you see he has
burrowed under his blanket   returned to the
unconscious   As for you there are bills
to pay   books to return to the library   food
to prepare and clothes to sort from a pile
on the floor   Snake will sleep for weeks
slipped from his skin to carry directives in
six directions   O do not let your serpent
die of thirst!   Without him we are like
stones strewn haphazardly over a plain   or
brutalized idiots massed on islands bereft
because we have not thought of bridges

Snowqueen

Snow is blowing horizontally as he drives
His headlights cutting into the flurry effect
a frenzy of fission   He grips the wheel
plunging into the dizzying swirl   helpless now
in his surging desire — rather the way after
all these years   he enters his wife's body

At twelve he'd coaxed PattySue to a cave — she'd
trembled as if she would freeze to death as
he'd lifted her dress   And lovely Louise
queen of the bayou   her sinuous back stretched
along the felt of her daddy's billiard table
that summer it had seemed too hot to move

No other lights on the road   all blindingly
white beyond the finite wedge of his beams —
he tears his gaze away from the gorgeous funnel
Sometimes   he knows   his wife grows weary of
his ardor   but she has learned to lie for him
like wheatfields under a Kansas sky and he
can never cover all of it   never   ever

Layered snow is flying so fast he slows to
a crawl   Silence in dense molecular shapes
packs his ear   She'd carried her babies
like sacks of grain   though the unborn   he
muses   may be more like blossoms floating in water
or air   Sex for him is supreme projection —
rocket slicing through outer space — and return :
grain of salt rocked in the womb of the sea

He crawls to the shoulder of the road and sits
with the engine pulsing through metal curving
around him — wipers off lights dimmed drowning
in her hot swirling skirts

Fire

Your new husband touches your wrist
Through 30,000 feet of blackness golden globes
burn the Amazon jungle   Clearing fires
your pilot explains : natives down there have
never seen a car or a book or a rockstar
Sparks leaping from chest to brain you are
leaving time   soaring from node to sunken node
of prehistoric light

Profferring cocktails the stewardess squeezes
among you   You want to hear ice cubes clacking
in summer glasses   but each passenger swallows
his fear   there is not a sound   speech has not
been deciphered here   you are dust particles
bound to a star falling sideways pale across
the heavens

You are twenty   your husband a few years older
and now you see that his life is a club he uses
to beat back his death   Your tongue lies
bloated inside your mouth — you wish for a koan
or someone beside you who knew how to weep

Stranded in space weighting yourselves with
Argentinean beef   chewing in unison   sloshing
mouthfuls with slugs of scotch — yet
no one is able to swallow   A baby shrieks
in the back of the plane   single unwavering
bonfires wasting the blackness

Your husband hails the stewardess for a cup
of coffee   The square line of his Aryan jaw
alarms you   He starts to explicate U.S.-Brazilian
relations — safe in his body he sees the plane
fueled by the dollar and guided by upright
intention spinning the thread which binds it
all together

He opens *The New York Times*   No one travels
beside you   In unearthly silence you feel yourself
blasting through plastic window and diving
into the flame   Somewhere a lamb is bleating
Which way to go : up or down   backwards or forwards
to live forever in mollusk molds or to die
by primordial fire?

Nuclear Orchards
(for Chris Grey)

    And then one of the children reaching up
grabs a handful of blossoms tossing them into
the air...
                they flutter down
                              he laughs
                                        you
catch it and move as a body clutching fistfuls
of appled cloud fluffed thick above you casting them
into the sweet spring
                        while ringing your field
of moon and flower the grownups stand like stones
in the dusk drinking and talking

In this way you sway in a flurry of scent lunging
and wheeling perfumes groundswirling under your
feet radish and cucumber close in the gardens pushing
through fertile ground

                      1956 : Nikita Khrushchev
has torn off his shoe and rapped it on the United
Nations conference table   Radioactive strontium-
90 is blowing on winds from atomic tests in Russia
and here in America settling into the teeth and
bones of everyone's children

From time to time the grownups discuss dis-
patching a certain ambassador into your magic
circle demanding what do you think you are doing—
tearing at the beautiful trees and shrieking
like banshees? You spin beyond them in mythic

silence   kicking your shoes off   tearing your
socks   grass drenched in apple juices   and moon
splashing sensate phrases into your fluttering arms —
in spangled dreams and summer attics you've practiced
this grand geometry for millenia
                                          The Soviets shot
our man Powers down from the sky   (later he said
a voice inside forbade him to bite the cyanide
bullet)   and some of your neighbors had bomb shelters
built like root canals under their orchards

At last Aunt Dorothy
                              tanned in her yellow dress
reluctantly enters your blaze of trees   charging
you all with wild and wanton behavior   They
call you indoors   handing you bowls of homemade
strawberry ice cream and send you back for
your shoes
                  while under the howling May heavens
the dogs bound off after rabbits — how grateful
you are for animals!

One by one each neighboring child drops late
into bed
              whispering to God :   *tonight we heard*
the off-key music   it tasted of apples   umbrellas
of blossoms whirling around us like giant anemones
trillions of petals crashing and bursting forever
inside us   and ever   around us   and ever   and
ever amen

Virginity

You go to him with your unbroken beauty
and stories belying your fear   His words in
another language rain over your desert
His hands on your breasts are blind men
seeing   Your eyelids catch fire   He sees
you have waited and even prayed and perhaps
you are ready : the heart must be cut and
lifted   steaming   up to the sun   He says
there is pain in the first sharp break and
then you are changed and ardent among women
The warsong rattling out of his chest thrusts
you into battle   You ride in front of him
facing backwards   spears and arrows passing
through flesh which parts to receive them

Returned to the body beside a river your
captor is crouching low on the bank listening
to stones   You sip the water he brings in
his hands   Where have you been?   Where will you
go together?   His phrases trailing off at the
ends describe a warrior ranging out — he
has torn you away from your village   your
father lies dying   he can't take you with him —
pray to the axis of river and sky erupted
within!

He rides away while you hide in your hands

After a time you are tugged from shore and swept
downstream   buoyed by this emptiness glowing
high inside you

Between the Eyes

At four in the morning you wake from a dream —
a child's face shocked with sight — strip off
your drenched nightshirt and move around the house
turning off lights   You lock the side door
And a grown man had wept   nervously touching
his streaming cheeks for the jammed heart
of his father   The air cuts a path for your
swimming skin   In the rippled mirror above the
sink   the tops of your breasts rise to express
emphatic life

Darkest blossoms in rivers and earth howl
in your dreams to be tendered   A feminine way
of receiving for which you have learned at
last to feed the beast without losing an arm
Leavetaking swallowed up half of your lifetime
detained as if by the grip of an infant or
dreams of men stretched to overexposure
You stand   you think   on the edge of your
lowland prepared to possess it — but wait!
The turgid press and swell of your breasts
cracks the glass

You climb into bed   chilled hands exploring
the evidence : conception against the will
after forty years of obedience to the body?
Your children's global faces float before you
Doggedly you pursue the shadow   closing in
again and again on the tiger's dissolving stripes
No use — your hands cup the water

Bureau and chairs are reassembling in unflinching
light   You tuck your head in your arms   "So"
You can only choose what has chosen you with
all the love you can muster

Breakage

When the life that has chosen you cracks
in two   you sail loose in its blood referring
to physics and intuition   Now you may call
something God   You phone your relations to
say goodbye   surfacing upside-down with dragons
smoking under your clothes

Galileo you went too far   They banished your
breakthrough and you revolved through infinite
octaves of fire and ice   We follow you off
the edge of the world shrieking for bread—
for madness   rain   creation   release   and parades
of mechanical roses

Gorgeously fractured the stone you have chosen
splits at the center   crashing the falls   Your
lifelong efforts to save yourself advise you
to stay in suspense   Once you hit bottom it's clear
all along superior forces assembled your particled
light   In moments of crisis something shifts
birth tearing body from body   stone cracks
the will is broken   flesh folding back away from
the bone   your galaxy imploding

Sixteen Tons

For thirty-five years a woman measures her
heaviness   She sees her soul as a bucket of dirt
to be emptied and filled again on the best of
days   She says to her husband   All day long
you strain in the attic drafting your castles so
that by night you have nothing to put in my bucket
but a spoonful or two of earth   With you so frugal
how is my life to round out?

Her husband is a poet   His bones are frozen
matchsticks   the beard shapes his head into a
perfect diamond   He has no response to this about
dirt   He looks across at her but his eyes are
marbles rolling away   When getting up and walking
into the kitchen she sighs once and for all
the breath rushing out of her is his punishment

Poor woman   he thinks   she longs to sit with
denizens of the world around a table eating butter
and boiled potatoes   when all I want is to go on
building secret doors that open and close without
a sound

In the kitchen   her children feeding on
meatloaf   the woman abruptly wonders if a bucket
of dirt flung about and a teaspoonful carefully
measured   isn't a misleading metaphor for what
she wants   What is truly empty   she thinks
stirring   doesn't want filling

Dionysus

When the god comes flying through your village
his timing is already perfect   You're up
to the elbow in washing   your husband
has taken the donkey to market   you're turning
exhausted soil   your womb resembles volcanic
ash   you've settled the little ones in their
hammocks and wound the wool on its skein
A moon full in cerulean skies tugs at the roots
of your hair   His singing drives through your pores
like arrows   you stand in the fields   you rise
from the loom   meal drops from flying fingers
feet spin under the threshold   olive trees
trailing with grasping hands as you race away
from the village

                        Cyclonic women converge
at the foot of the mountain — behind his body
a channel unfolding   weightless you are
inhaled up the passage   his bestial laugh
breaks from your throats and no one remembers the decades
of labor   loping through quicksilver dusk as one
body   sun somersaulting through flaming
hoops   pelvis and breastbone flags unfurling
the god exhaling his piercing whistle   you rise
on those notes   your lungs blown open   voices
stampeding toward crescendo — *my god you deliver us
stretched to the limit we always knew you
would come*

Gratitude

Bursting out of the blue seas of your
afternoon   dispersing like beautiful birds
images fly from the tip of his tongue
red sun (you can't quite remember)
inflaming its bed   conifers bleeding
over the hills behind the house you feel
yourself lifting and curving around him
again and again breaking against his body
His pores open like tiny doors inside
his clothes   In you take him   into the
clotted redblack soil of ancestor blood
millions of rivulets   human and animal
merging inside you

When wind stops ringing green from trees
and rocks roll apart in the water   when
light bends away from the glass   oh
what will become of this strange music?
Gratitude blooms in cumulus shapes   something
the blind woman knows   you imagine   learning
the slope of the ground through her cane
undulant warmth of mudded walls raking
the tips of her fingers

Longing

Three saints live by the river and you
among them   Sandbanked beside the rolling
water   two by two inclined to couple   their
spirits are clear and glistening like fish

You look at your mate   a kind and deliberate
being   sitting or standing or ferrying pilgrims
his movement issues from stillness   Other men
moved like discreet animals — not like water
like this one

Among them still you do not comprehend the
divine nature of love   You offer yourself
this truth : one man becomes the next in you —
he moves on a certain tensile strength   a
sweetness drawn from the mother   or maybe
his twisted longing   You feed on his strength
but forsake him for weakness   And still you
long to twine the trunk   rough in its bark pressing
against it   throbbing above the root

Your saints live free from this intertwining
like plants taking rain   sun   night on the
same hillside   Deranged snipers   ruined teachers
ticking off months to retirement in stultifying
lunchrooms   the President's men hoarding deadly
warheads — these are your mothers and brothers
their dreams are your bloodstream   belly down
you go dragging your bones around the temple
idiot girl expanding with life you never knew
you were making   Here in this place you can't

deny it   You've loved Hotei in the Japanese
scroll   peering over his bulbous bag   huge as
a hillock   grinning out like a fool   Leave it
behind   your inheritance smashes you flat : here
is your transformation

You kneel by your saint   You tell him you want
to return to the world   He touches your hair
From an axis of rape and misconception your
planet struggles for justice   for faith   in itself
and its death   Rivers   saints   warmongers
fools — you carry them forward inside you

Sending the Body Out *was set
in 12 point Schneidler. It was printed by
Thomson-Shore on acid-free paper and the binding
sewn for book longevity.*

*Twenty-five copies of an edition of 1000
are signed and numbered by
the poet and artist.*